Copyright Inf

Copyright © 2017 by Lee De ed
worldwide. CoachPrincetonBask

No part of this publication may d,
or given away in any form without the prior written consent of the author/publisher or the terms relayed to you herein.

This book not authorized by Bill Self or Kansas basketball, but it mirrors some of the same actions they use to dominate the Big 12 each year.

Foreword

The Kansas Multiple Option Basketball System is a complete offensive encyclopedia. If you have good post players focus on the high/low options and if your guards are your best players then spend more time on the Ball Screen Motion.

Also included is a Universal Press Offense that any team can use to break pressure defenses for layups and points.

Also, visit my website for **more information** and **free handouts** about my favorite offensive system by visiting CoachPrincetonBasketball.com. Thank you again, and best of luck to you this season!

Lee DeForest
@coachdeforest
coachdeforest@gmail.com

Table of Contents

Chapter 1 7
Kansas Motion Offense 7
Wing Entry with Post at Top of Key 12
Weak Side Down Screen Action 13
Weak Side Screen Setup and Reads 14
High/Low Motion Weak Side Cut Continuity 15
High/Low Motion Strong Side Cut Continuity 17

Chapter 2 19
Counters and Entries 20
Pressure Release Counter 21
Point Dribble Entry 23

Chapter 3 25
Breakdown Drills 25
Backcut Layups 26
Skip Pass Shooting 26
Double Down Drill 26
Stagger Screen Drill 27
Wing Down Screen Drill 27
High Low Post Drill 27
Zipper Cut Drill 28
Ball Screen Breakdown Drill 28

Chapter 4 29
How to Beat Any Press Defense 29
1-3-1 Press Offense.. 30
Guard Entry 30
Screener Entry 32
Sideline Entry 33

Chapter 5 35
Kansas Ball Screen Continuity Offense 35
Bird.. 39
Under 40
Over 40
Buna 41
Weave 41
Push 5 42
X 42
Utah 43
LA 43
Corner 43
Post 44
In-Game Coaching "Cheat Sheet" 45

Conclusion 46
Additional Basketball Coaching Resources 47

Chapter 1

Kansas Motion Offense

The Kansas version of the 3-out/2-in motion offense is simplified with some basic rules. This offense is designed to pull one of the post players to the high post, allowing the other to be isolated in the low post with room to score. The offense also allows your perimeter players to score off the catch or dribble with the look of a true motion offense. This offense provides the traditional advantages of a motion offense while adding structure to keep personnel in their high percentage scoring areas.

Why is this offense different?

True motion offense is difficult and time consuming to teach. This motion is more structured, but has the same components as a true motion offense that make it hard to scout. Those components include:

- Ball screens
- Staggered screens
- Double screens
- Big-Little screens
- Cross screens
- Back screens
- Dribble penetration
- Inside-Out opportunities

This hi-low motion offense is designed for post players who are not great perimeter shooters. Based on these rules, the offense should not require post players to receive a pass outside of their scoring range. Also, it does not put players in a position to shoot a defended shot outside of the paint. This high/low offense is a very simple offense.

How to Coach the Kansas Multiple Option Basketball System

Coach Bill Self once claimed that while at Tulsa he installed the offense in only 4 days before defeating a team ranked in the top 25. This offense is predicated on:

- Point to wing entry pass
- Point to high post entry pass
- Point to wing dribble entry

Initial Positioning Diagram

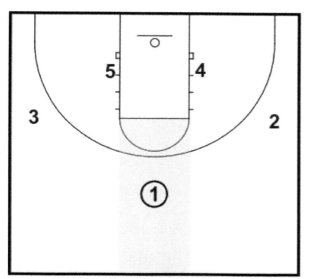

The 1 should enter the offense within the lane line extended.

Wings set up near the free throw line extended.

High/Low Motion Weak Side Guard Cut

High/Low 5 and 4 Post Screening Action

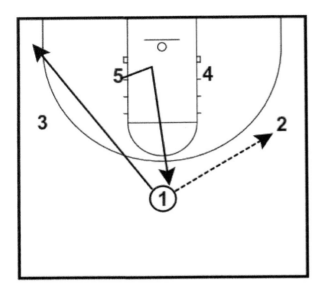

1 passes to 2 and cuts to weak side corner.

5 flashes to top of key.

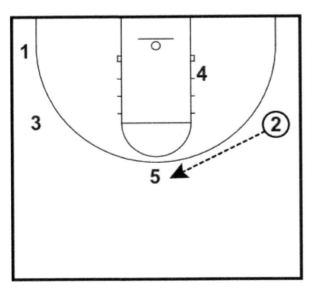

2 passes to 5

Ideal location is at the elbow

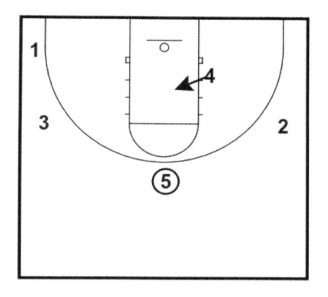

When the high post has the ball, the low post will be in a direct line between the ball and the basket. This will force the defender to commit to a defensive position (front, behind, side). If the post does not move in a direct line with the ball and basket, he is easier to defend.

How to Coach the Kansas Multiple Option Basketball System

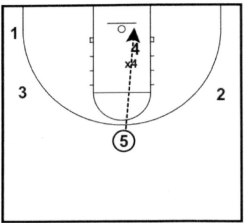 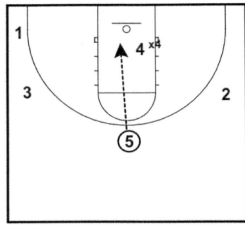

Lob versus a front

Teach post to lock and seal with a reverse pivot in the post to create the angle. The post player waits until the ball is directly above their head before releasing to catch basketball. The passer should make an overhead pass near the corner of the backboard for the proper angle.

Bounce pass after seal

Teach post to seal and wait for the first bounce before releasing to grab the basketball with two hands then pivot to score. Passer should make the pass where the defense can't get it and it should be a bounce pass.

Wing Entry with Post at Top of Key

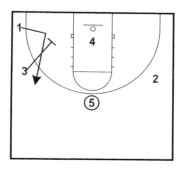

1 will set up defender for a downscreen from 3.

4 will continue to seal and work inside.

5 passes to 1.

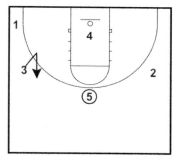

3 will replace cut or v-cut to get open on the wing.

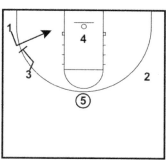

3 will screen down on the wing, but 1 will slip the screen for a backcut. The passing window is small, but if the 4 does a good job of sealing, the help will not be there. 3 will replace cut back to the wing if the pass is not made on the slip cut.

Weak Side Down Screen Action

When coaches talk about strong side and weak side, they are referring to the location of the ball in relation to the scoring action. A scoring action can be a ball screen or post up or isolation, but in this offense, we are referring to the down screening action away from the basketball. This eliminates any help depending on the location and angle of the screen.

In the example below, it is easy to see the large area that is created behind the defense for the ball to be passed into the post. The defense must choose to defend the post and leave the screener/cutter action alone or defend the screening action. We will examine some of the options on the weak side.

Remember, you can determine where you want the weak side screen to happen; Kansas screens around the elbow.

Weak Side Screen Setup and Reads

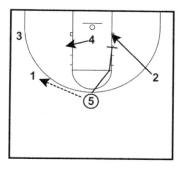

On the pass to the 1, the offense moves into weakside screening action between the 5 and 2.

There are several reads that the offense can make depending on how the defense plays the cut from the 2.

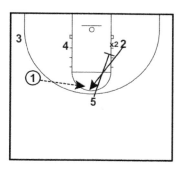

Straight Cut

To stay in the continuity or the simplest read for the offense to make off the screen.

The 2 looks for the shot off the down screen.

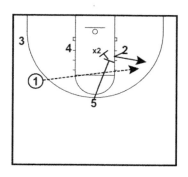

Fade Cut

If the defender, X2, plays inside the screen near the rim, then the simplest cut is for the 2 to fade cut away from the ball as the screener also changes position on the screen. A skip pass can be thrown to 2 for the shot or drive against X2's closeout.

Curl Cut

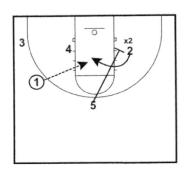

If X2 plays behind or tight on the offense, then the 2 will setup a little more off the lane and the 5 will set a hard screen.

The 2 can curl hard off the screen into the lane for the pass and score.

High/Low Motion Weak Side Cut Continuity

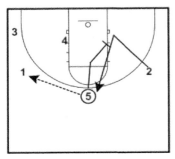

Continued on the 5 to 1 swing pass if the 2 does not read the screen by 5.

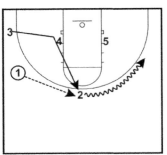

1 reverses to 2.

2 will dribble enter to the wing to get an angle for the 5.

3 cuts to fill the top of the key.

1 stays wide.

RULE: Guard dribble enters to a wing will be followed by corner player sprinting to top of key.

4 and 5 High/Low Continuity

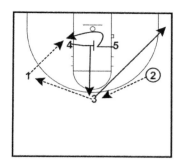

On the pass from 2 to 3 to 1, the ball is reversed. 3 cuts to the opposite corner.

4 screens across for 5 to the post and 5 cuts under the screen. 4 fills the top.

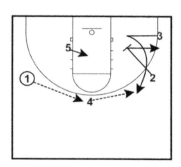

1 reverses to 4 and 5 will look for the high/low pass from 4.

2 downscreens for the 3.

3 cuts to wing if no read off the down screen from 2.

5 follows the ball and posts up hard.

Same action and reads as before between the 4 and 1.

1 cuts to the top of the key.

3 reverses to 1 at the top of the key.

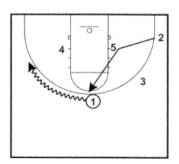

1 dribble enters to the wing for the 4 to get a better angle.

2 fills the top of the key.

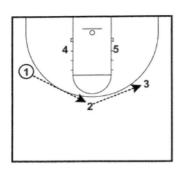

1 passes to 2 and we are in the same motion as before in our High/Low Motion. (See **Continuity**)

High/Low Motion Strong Side Cut Continuity
Stagger Screen for Passer Option

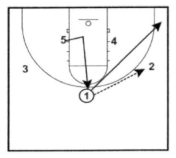

1 passes to 2 and cuts to strong side corner.

5 cuts to top of the key.

2 passes to 5 at top of key.

4 seals for high/low pass from 5.

How to Coach the Kansas Multiple Option Basketball System

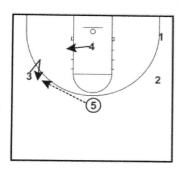

3 gets open on the wing and 5 passes to 3.

4 follows the ball and seals.

3 looks inside to 4.

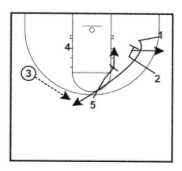

On the pass from 5 to 3, the 5 and 2 set a stagger screen for 1.

5 sets the screen near the elbow, and the 2 head hunts for 1.

1 sprints off the screens looking for a shot at the top of the key.

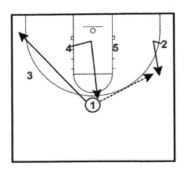

This is the basic 3 out/2 in motion set.

Reset with the guards on the perimeter and the 5 and 4 in the posts.

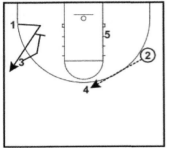

The motion continues with either a strong side or weak side cut which triggers the motion.

Chapter 2
Counters and Entries

Teams will try to pressure you and force you to make plays instead of run an offense as effective as this one. That is a common tactic at every level of basketball. When you begin to teach this offense and develop your players to the point they are effective, then you should expect teams to try and take away your first pass across half court.

If your team is not prepared for this change in tactics by the defense then you will be caught off guard. There are some simple and effective counters to defensive pressure that you should teach your players to use once you have the basic motion offense installed.

Pressure Release Counter

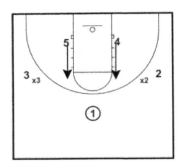

When the defense denies the wing entry pass, both post players will flash to the elbows and both wing players will move to a position where they will be higher than the ball on the post entry pass.

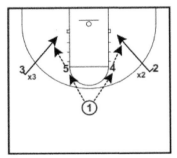

The first option is a back cut by the ball side wing. The post will drop step in the direction of the pass and use a bounce pass to feed the cutter. The wing will start the cut by pivoting on the back foot and stepping across the defender and placing him on his back or hip.

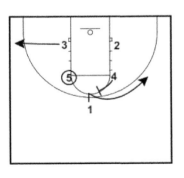

If back cut is not open, the 3 will widen to the corner. The 2 stays on the block. 4 flare screens for 1 and pops out to elbow extended.

Coaching Point: *This is a good post play for the 2 since there is no help.*

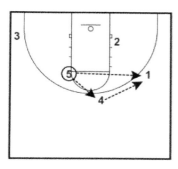

5 passes to 4 and then 4 to 1.

5 can also pass to 1 on the flare screen.

4 and 5 will double down screen for 2. This can be an elevator screen set for the 2 to the top of the key.

1 passes to 2 for the shot.

Coaching Point: *1 can also drive to the basket after 2 cuts off the screen since the bigs are lifted high.*

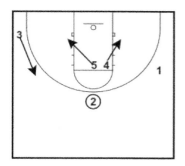

If shot or drive is not available, then we are back in the motion offense.

Point Dribble Entry

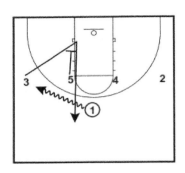

The players have gone through the pressure release cuts and have filled the elbows.

1 dribbles to a wing as 3 cuts to block and 5 sets a down screen for 3 to cut up the lane line.

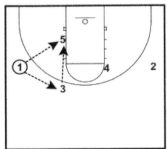

1 can pass to 5 for an easy score inside or pass to 3 for the high/low.

1 passes to 3 if 5 is not open.

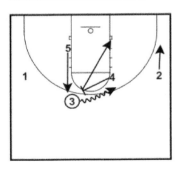

As ball is in the air to 3, the 4 is moving to set the ball screen.

3 will drive off the ball screen as 2 relocates for spacing.

5 flashes to the top as 3 drives off the screen set by 4.

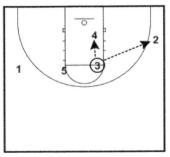

3 will look for the layup or hit the 4 on the roll.

If 2's defender helps on 3's drive then 2 will be open for the shot.

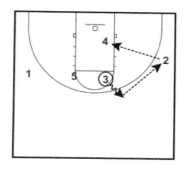

If there is a switch between 4 and 3, then 3 will pass to the wing and into the post for the 4.

There is a mismatch inside.

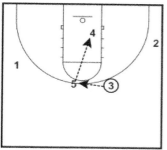

3 drives to the basket and if there is a switch, then the 3 can reverse back to the 5 for the high/low with 4.

This works well against the switch on the ball screen.

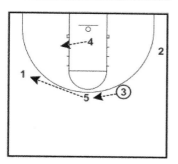

Continue the offense by reversing the ball from 3 to 5 to 1.

Then there would be a 5 and 3 stagger screen for the 2.

4 follows the ball to post up.

Chapter 3

Breakdown Drills

Breakdown drills that teach the basic motion of the offense are critical to teach players how to read a defense instead of playing like robots, mindlessly walking from one spot on the court to another. We have all seen teams improve their offense during the season. One of the most critical components to improving is installing the offense first, breaking down the components of the offense, and then practicing the offense from the beginning. This is called the whole-part-whole method of instruction and it is used at all levels of the game in many different sports to teach team actions and the timing necessary to be effective.

Always remember that offense is more difficult to teach than defense and do not underestimate the amount of practice time it will take, early in the season, to fully prepare your offense for the game speed cuts and decisions your players will need to learn how to make. One thing you can always do as a coach is to run an offense continuously as opposed to scoring the first option so that your players learn the cuts and spacing first then teach the different reads for the players to make after they learn the motion.

General Drill Rules:

1. Shoot for either a time or number of makes for each drill.
2. Use each drill during the week to break down the specific teaching points of each play.
3. Use a previous practice or scrimmage session to inform your staff about what to look for during these drills.

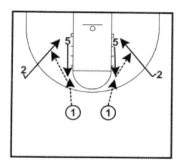

Backcut Layups

Guards in lines at the elbow extended and wings at the free throw extended and posts at the block.

Practice the backcuts and timing and passing angles with different finishes on the catch.

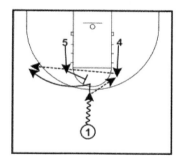

Skip Pass Shooting

1 passes to either elbow and practices the flare screen and skip pass. Work on the timing and speed of the cuts after the elbow entry pass.

Guard will shoot on the pass and posts will reset.

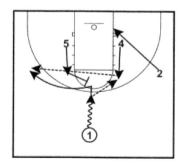

Double Down Drill

Add one more guard to the wing and after the elbow entry pass the flare screen is set for the guard.

The post will pass from the elbow to the wing.

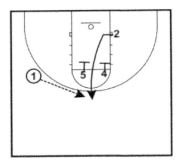

On the pass to the guard after the flare screen, the other guard will cut between the posts for an elevator screen or a double screen set shoulder to shoulder.

A 4 or 5 can also practice slipping the screen for the pass.

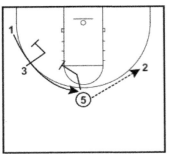

Stagger Screen Drill

Start with a post with the ball up top and work on the post and wing setting a stagger screen for the shooter in the corner. Rotate posts and guards.

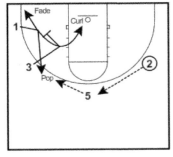

Wing Down Screen Drill

Wing reverses to post up top and wing will down screen for the corner player.

Work on the pop, curl, and fade cut on the down screen and passes.

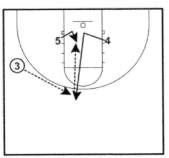

High Low Post Drill

Can use a coach for the passer, but the 5 will work on sealing and the 4 will flash to the top of the key.

The wing reverses to the 4 and we work on the pass to the 5.

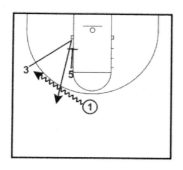

Zipper Cut Drill

Guard will have the ball up top and practice a dribble entry to the wing while the wing backcuts and 5 downscreens for the 3.

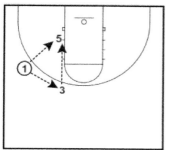

Guard either passes to the post for a score and practices the post entry pass or passes to the 3 at the top and we work on the high/low pass between the 3 and the 5.

Ball Screen Breakdown Drill

Start with the ball on the wing and pass to the 3 while the 4 works on the screen and roll with the guard.

5 will fill the top of the key on the ball screen by the 4.

Also work on 3 reversing the ball to the 5 for the high/low pass between the 5 and 4.

Work on different entry passes between the 5 and 4.

Chapter 4

How to Beat Any Press Defense

A good press defense can totally destroy any good offense. There is little reason to practice a half-court offense and work on execution when a team faces a good pressing defense and finds itself unprepared. If your team cannot force the opponent into "playing basketball" or choosing to defend your team in the half court, then there is little reason to focus on execution of a half court system. This is why most coaches say that in the post season, the press is less effective because during the struggles of the season, your team has probably faced every imaginable type of defense. It is naïve to think that your team will not face a full court press during the season, and you must prepare, Day 1, on the proper fundamentals and spacing necessary to defeat any type of press. Our drill book on reducing turnovers is here.

There is a reason, considering the way the rules are interpreted today, that full court pressing teams rarely win the championships. There are cases where the talent level is so diluted that pressing teams will win, but in the best leagues, at the most competitive levels, there are few examples of championship pressing teams. Does that mean your team should not prepare? No!

The basic rules for any press offense is to always have 3 outlets and one long pass available against trap. If possible, keep the ball centered in the full court, but it is critical to center the ball after the initial full court press has been defeated. **In other words, get the ball across half court preferably without using the dribble and then immediately instruct your players to get the basketball into the center of the court in case a team traps late.** The sideline is a pressing team's best friend.

1-3-1 Press Offense

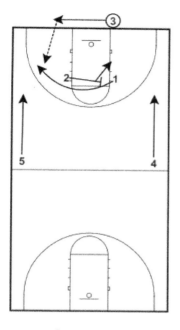

Guard Entry

2 screens for 1 as 3 runs the baseline. The baseline run is not required, but makes the inbounds pass more effective against teams that have a defender on the inbounder. It is easier because it changes the angle for the defenders making it more difficult to pressure the inbounds pass.

5 and 4 sprint to free throw line extended. 3 looks deep for 4 and 5, but inbounds the ball to a guard.

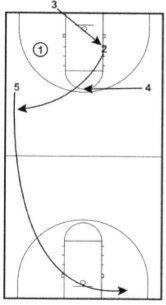

1 will first look up the sideline and then reverse the ball to the 3.

The 2 will sprint under the 1 while the 4 sprints to the middle for the pass. 5 clears out and works to stay opposite the ball.

The other 4 players work to keep the player with the ball the option of 3 outlets.

Against a man to man full court press, the ballhandler will wave and clear out the remaining offensive players to bring the ball up 1 on 1.

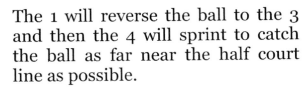

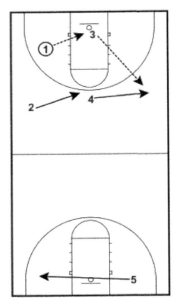

The 1 will reverse the ball to the 3 and then the 4 will sprint to catch the ball as far near the half court line as possible.

The 2 will cut hard to the middle on the pass from the 1 to 3 and 3 will look for 2 for the pass.

The 5 stays opposite the ball when it is on the sideline.

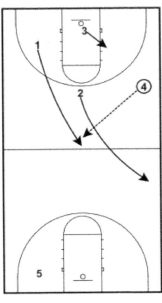

The 4 will look up the sideline for the 2 and then pass to the 1 in the middle to create a fast break situation. The 5 will be ready to score the layup while the 2 will fill the outside lane.

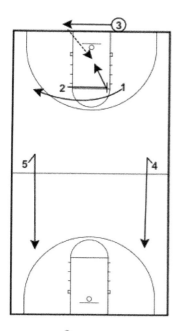

Screener Entry

The screener will flash to the ball after the screen for the 1. The 4 and 5 will rotate back quickly to create space.

This works against good defensive pressure denying the 1.

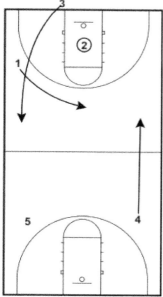

The screener, the 2, has the ball in the middle of court. The 1 will banana cut to the middle of the court and the 5 will stay opposite the ball while the 4 sprints high.

The 3 will replace the cut from the 1.

This will create the 1-3-1 set that makes this press break effective.

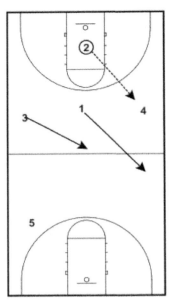

If the 1 is not open, the 4 should be open and 2 will pass the ball to the 4.

On the pass to the 4, the 1 will cut sideline and immediately behind 1's cut, the 3 will fill the middle.

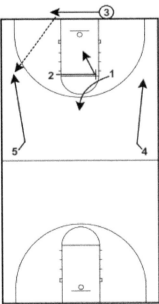

Sideline Entry

This can be a play call by the coach or a read by the players.

The defense will deny the 1 and 2 while the 4 and 5 cut hard to the free throw line extended.

The 3 will pass to either sideline post entry against pressure.

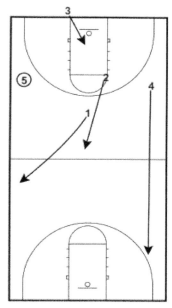

On the pass to the 5, the 1 will dive immediately down the floor. The idea is that the defense has denied the guards, and this pass will open up your best ball handler in the middle of the court.

The 4 will sprint back to fill a lane and if the 1 is denied, the 2 will follow the cut with a second hard cut down the middle. This cut is always open.

The 1 will fill a sideline and this will create a fast break situation.

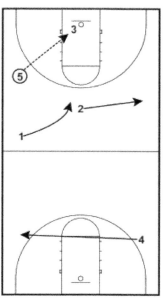

If the 1 and 2 are not open on their cuts, the 5 will reverse to the 3.

We are in our press offense at this point, and the 1 cuts middle as the 2 fills the sideline. The 4 will work to stay opposite the ball.

Chapter 5

Kansas Ball Screen Continuity Offense

In the Kansas Ball Screen Offense, the 4 and 5 will screen for the perimeter players positioned on the high wing, wing, or corner. The 3 perimeter players are interchangeable and the 2 post players are also. The offense is initiated when the 1 passes to either wing and then cuts to either corner. Once this pass and cut has been made, we are in the offense.

The basic rules for the post players are important for this offense. After all, a ball screen based offense will not be effective without a proper screen and set up technique. While there are many opinions on how to set a screen and the proper angle to roll to the rim, the most important consideration in this action should be whether a screen gets the guard open or not. In effect, every ball screen should create a bad hedge or uncertainty in the defense.

Here are 3 basic rules for ball screeners to be effective:

1. The screener must create separation from the defender so that the defense can't make a good hedge or double team.

2. The 4 or 5 that goes to screen is determined by their defender. Send the post that has a defender that cannot hedge well.

3. If both defenders are good, have 5 screen for 4 to free him.

In a game, a good coaching adjustment is to target the slower defender, the lazy defender, or the one in foul trouble.

There are some general rules for the perimeter and post players in this offense. The point guard, 2 guard, and small forward, must have a good understanding of their defender's position when they get the ball.

The perimeter players must set their defenders up after they get the ball by:

- kick off the defense (jab step hard at the defender or in the opposite direction from the screen)
- reverse pivoting
- kick off defender, reverse pivot, fake and go
- back down dribble into wing position
- pass fake or shot fake

Remember, perimeter plays must not run towards the ball screen action as it occurs and instead occupy the defense with their spacing. One other coaching point to keep in mind is try and create bad help by repositioning on the weak side if the defense tries to help.

The goal is to win each possession in order to win the game. As a coach, it is important to teach the players their responsibilities and the reasons for their movements. A coach should inform each player of their individual strengths and weaknesses. Shooters need to create space, drivers need to attack off the screens, and post players need to duck in hard. Also, coaches should instruct players on the specific shots that are best for each player based on defender's strengths and weaknesses as well as the time and score.

As for post players in this offense, each screen should be set at a good angle. The most common error made by screeners is releasing the screen set for the ball handler too soon. A screener must set and hold the screen to create space off the dribble for the perimeter player. This timing creates a "pocket" to receive the pass from the guard. As the post player sprints out to screen, a coach should teach the concept of separation and creating bad hedges by changing the angle of the screen late and interchanging with the other post. This will be explained more fully. Finally, the post player must understand how and when to slip a ball screen against an aggressive trap or hedge. The post player has a few reads that should be reinforced and know how to read their defender.

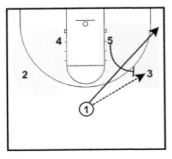

The offense is initiated when the 1 passes to either wing and then cuts to either corner. Once this pass and cut has been made, we are in the offense. The 4 and 2 play together to create a shot while the 1, 3, and 5 create a triangle on the strong side.

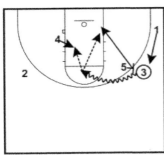

The basic motion is a side screen and roll by a post followed by the other post reading the defense and the other perimeter reading the play also. If the 1 cuts ballside then it is an automatic fill behind on the post player's roll to the basket.

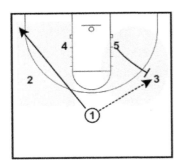

If the 1 cuts to the weak side to form a weak side triangle, the 5 and 3 play to create a shot on the strong side.

How to Coach the Kansas Multiple Option Basketball System

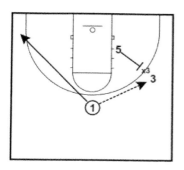

A good angle for the 5 to screen for the 3 is right behind the 3 and basically a back screen. This gives the 3 the option to drive either way off the ball screen.

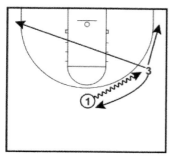

If the 1 can't pass to the 3 on the wing, then the 3 can clear out to the weak side or strong side or even fill the top. The fill the top option is rarely used, but would be to place the 3 in the high wing position for a pass back from 1.

Here are the 3 places for the ball screen to be set by the post for the guard. The high wing, wing, and corner stress the defense in different ways and should be mixed up to keep the defense off balance and take advantage of matchups.

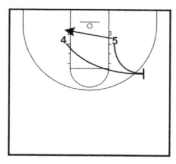

The posts have options also. The 5 can immediately screen for the wing or an interchange with 4 is possible. Again, matchups and variation will determine the best option.

How to Coach the Kansas Multiple Option Basketball System

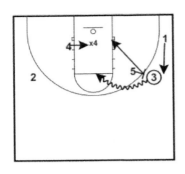

Now that we understand some of the basic options, let's talk about the reads for the weak side post, 4.

If the defender on the 4, X4, plays midline then we want a hard duck in and seal as the 3 attacks the lane.

Coaching Tip: 4 will seal for the score *or* to prevent the X4 from helping on the drive.

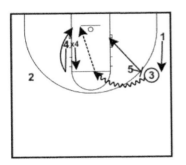

If the X4 plays tight on the 4 or to change up the angles, the 4 will cut to the elbow and back cut for the lob if the defense overplays.

Walk the defender up the lane and then change directions for the lob.

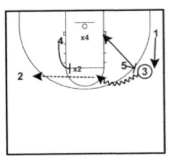

If the 4 reads the X2 helping in the lane to stop the drive, then the 4 will set a fade screen for the 2 and then look to post in the lane or slip the screen.

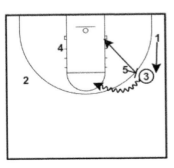

Bird

The 3 will drive hard off the screen by 5. To force a pass back to 1, we call it a "Larry Bird" for "look back" so in a game we can say, "Bird the wing" to call this action.

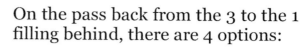

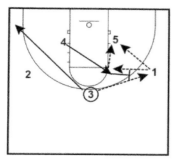

On the pass back from the 3 to the 1 filling behind, there are 4 options:

1. Shoot the 3
2. Feed the low post
3. Pass to the 4 for the high/low
4. Wait for the 4 to ball screen

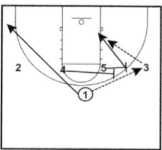

Under

Against teams that hedge hard or trap the ball screen, run this counter and move both posts to the elbows. They both sprint to screen at the same time, but the first post slips to the basket for a quick score.

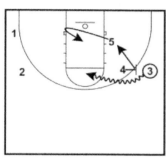

The second post sets the screen and we are in our normal ball screen action while the first post man goes to the opposite block to duck in on the pick and roll on the wing between the 4 and 3.

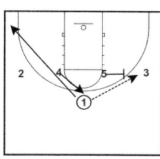

Over

This is another counter against teams that trap or hedge hard against the ball screen. Here, the first post sprints to screen like in Under, but the second post fills the high post for a quick pass.

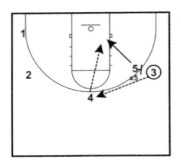

Instead of the 3 passing to the slip as in Under, the 3 will pass to the 4 for a pass over the top of the defense as the 5 slips to the rim.

This can be a lob pass.

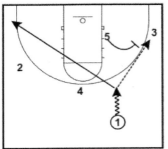

Buna

The first pass to the wing is closer to the corner, the 1 cuts opposite. 5 man is low and 4 man is high. The 5 steps out to screen for the 3.

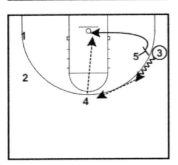

As the 3 comes off the ball screen, the pass is made to the 4 for the quick dump down pass from the 4 to the 5 on the roll to the rim.

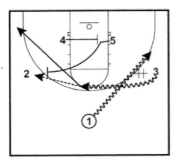

Weave

Use this call to start a dribble handoff with the ball handler and the wing. One reason to do this is to force a possible switch between the guards or to add variation to attack the rim off the handoff.

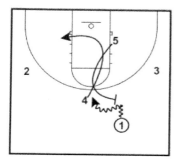

Push 5

This is a good play against pressure. We circle the 4 down in front of the 5 as the 5 sprints to ball screen for the 1.

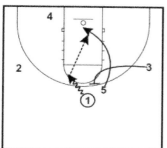

Timing is important here. As the 5 is moving to set the ball screen for the 1, the 3 is also moving (not showing screen) and 1 comes off the 5's ball screen as 3 back screens for the 5. Throw the lob to the 5 as the 4 seals the help defender.

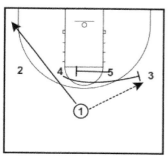

X

This is a great option to run the Under or Over action. It begins with a screen between the posts to create a switch or confusion. A simple adjustment that pays big rewards.

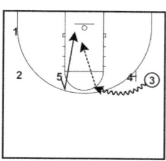

Now that we have had a post interchange at the high post, we immediately backcut the 5 as the 3 attacks off the ball screen by 4. Also, the 4 could change the angle of the ball screen to set a back screen.

Utah

This option will give you a quick score for the layup or 3 before you get into the ball screen motion. The 1 passes to 3 and sets a backscreen for the 4 as the 5 sets a down screen for the 2 cutting to the top.

LA

1 passes to the 3 and cuts off the 2 and 4 weak side double screen. The 5 sets a backscreen for the 1 and then a ball screen.

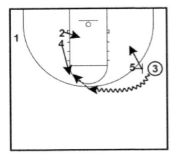

The focus here is on the 2 posting up a guard as the 3 comes off the ball screen and the 4 pops to the high post then tries to dump the ball into the 2 posting up.

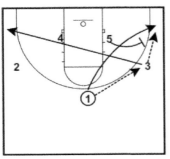

Corner

1 cuts to the ball side corner as in the normal ball screen action, but this time, 3 passes to 1 and clears weak side as the 5 steps out to screen. This is a good change up.

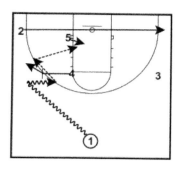

Post

1 dribbles to the wing as the 2 cuts over the top of the 5 to free them up in the post. 1 will drive hard off the side ball screen with 4 as 4 pops to receive the pass back from the 1 and feed the post 5.

In-Game Coaching "Cheat Sheet"

Controlling the location of the ball screens
High – high wing ball screen
T – wing ball screen
C – corner ball screen

Coaching the post players
Down – tells weak side post to duck in hard on all ball screens
Fox (Flare screen) – tells weak side post to stay high opposite elbow and set a flare screen
Flip (Setup for lob) – tells weak side post to stay high opposite elbow and goes for lob
Cross – tells post players to interchange or screen for each other before the wing screen is set

Quick Adjustments and Sets
Corner – motion starts with a wing to corner pass
Bird – stands for Larry Bird or look back after the ball screen is set and passes back
Post – quick post up call for the 5
X – sets up a high post interchange and a lob
Utah – quick call to get a score inside or a 3 point shot
LA – post up the 2 on the block
Weave – start the offense with a point to wing dribble weave
Push 5 – sets up a quick lob for your 5
Buna – start the offense with the 5 low and the 4 high
Over – set to attack a hard hedge or trap where the high post passes over on the slip
Under – set to attack a hard hedge or trap where first screener slips

Conclusion

"In practice, don't just run basketball drills, teach the players how to play basketball." - Meyer, Don

One of the reasons that I wanted to share this information with you is because there is so much information out there for coaches. There are tons of drills out there that have goal or basis in basketball, but coaches do them anyway. What I hope to provide you is something that is fundamental in nature and fits within any system.

I hope as a coach you are never finished learning and continue to develop your coaching knowledge to share it with other coaches. That is what this game is all about, and we all share with one another. On that note, if you enjoyed this book, **please leave a review and share your thoughts**. I would really appreciate it and plan to release more books in the future.

Thank you and good luck!

Lee DeForest

coachdeforest@gmail.com

http://coachprincetonbasketball.com

Additional Basketball Coaching Resources

Youth Basketball Coaching Drills

Turnovers eBook on Amazon

Princeton Offense System Preview

Princeton Offensive System Review

Printed in Great Britain
by Amazon